The Let's Talk Library™

Let's Talk About
Dyslexia

Melanie Apel Gordon

The Rosen Publishing Group's
PowerKids Press™
New York

This book is dedicated to my sister Mindy, who loves to read. Love, Melanie.

Published in 1999 by The Rosen Publishing Group, Inc.
29 East 21st Street, New York, NY 10010

First Edition

Book Design: Erin McKenna

Photo Credits: Cover photo, pp. 4, 7, 8, 11, 12, 15, 16, 20 by Donna Scholl; p.19 © Skjold Photographs.

Gordon, Melanie Apel.
   Let's talk about dyslexia / by Melanie Apel Gordon.
       p.   cm. — (The Let's talk library)
   Includes index.
   Summary: Discusses a learning disability of approximately one in every ten people, including Albert Einstein and Thomas Edison and how to cope with it.
   ISBN 0-8239-5199-5
   1. Dyslexia—Juvenile literature. 2. Dyslexic children—Education—Juvenile literature. [1. Dyslexia.]
I. Title. II. Series.
LB1050.5.G67 1998
371.91'44—dc21   97-44744
                                                                        CIP
                                                                         AC

Manufactured in the United States of America

Table of Contents

Mindy Can't Read

Every Friday Mindy's dad picks her up after school. On their way home, they always stop for a special treat. Mindy's favorite treat is ice cream. Mindy's dad picks a different kind of ice cream every week. Mindy always gets chocolate. Sometimes she wishes she could have a different kind. But Mindy can't read the list of choices. Mindy doesn't tell her dad that she has trouble reading. She doesn't want him to think that she isn't smart.

◀ Just because you have trouble reading doesn't mean that you are not smart.

Dyslexia

Some people have trouble reading because they have **dyslexia** (dis-LEK-see-uh). When kids have dyslexia, they may not see printed words correctly. They may have a hard time with reading, writing, math, or spelling. Some people who have dyslexia also have trouble keeping things **organized** (OR-guh-nyzd). They may often forget where they put things. A person who has dyslexia is called **dyslexic** (dis-LEK-sik).

Reading and writing can be confusing ▶
for someone with dyslexia.

Who Has Dyslexia?

Dyslexia is a **learning disability** (LER-ning dis-uh-BIL-uh-tee). It is not a sickness that you can catch. About one in every ten people in the United States has dyslexia. Doctors believe that the number of girls who have dyslexia is about the same as the number of boys who have it. Nobody knows exactly why some people are dyslexic and others aren't. It may be that certain parts of your brain don't grow as fast as others. Or maybe your brain works differently than other people's do.

◀ Kids with dyslexia enjoy the same activities as other kids.

Letters and Numbers

Some dyslexic people don't read letters and numbers the way other people do. Some letters may be in the wrong place in a word. A dyslexic person may read or write the letter **d** instead of **b.** Or they may see the word **sign** and think it says **sing.** Some dyslexic people have a hard time remembering which is their right hand and which is their left. Dyslexia is different for each person who has it.

Doctors used to think that whole words or sentences looked backwards to dyslexics. But many doctors no longer think this is true. ▶

Reading, Writing, and Math

Kids who have dyslexia can understand everything their teachers say. But it's hard for them to read books and do homework. Kids with dyslexia might have handwriting that's hard to read. Some dyslexics have trouble with numbers. Math is hard for them too. If they see the numbers in a math problem in the wrong order, their answers to the problem will be wrong. Kids who have a hard time with reading, writing, and math may not like school at all.

◀ Dyslexic kids often struggle with their classwork.

How Dyslexics Read and Write

Dyslexic kids may not remember the names of letters or the sounds that letters make. This makes it hard for them to understand what they are reading. Sometimes they may know which letters make a word but may have trouble remembering how to write the letters. Or they might forget the order in which the letters go. Dyslexic kids will often pretend that they can understand everything they read. They might listen to their friends talk about the stories they have read for school so they know what the stories are about.

Sometimes dyslexic kids will stop doing their schoolwork or try to get friends to do it for them. ▶

Trouble in School

Dyslexic kids often have trouble with school. But they may not tell their teachers that they are having trouble. So dyslexic kids try even harder to do their schoolwork correctly. But their work may be hard to read and their answers may be wrong. Teachers who don't know that these kids have a problem will just tell them to try harder. Dyslexic kids often get **frustrated** (FRUS-tray-ted). School is not much fun if you are having trouble. But if you're dyslexic, you're not alone.

◀ Tell your teacher if you are feeling frustrated in your class.

Getting Help

Tell your parents and teachers if you are having a hard time with reading, writing, or math. They can help you. There are special tests to **diagnose** (dy-ug-NOHS) dyslexia. And you can learn ways to read better. It will take time and hard work. But you can learn to read and write well. You can also use computers to write. This can make it easier for you to write down your thoughts and ideas.

Parents, teachers, and other grown-ups ▶ can help you practice reading.

Dyslexics Are Smart

Dyslexics may have trouble reading and writing, but that doesn't mean that they aren't smart. Most dyslexics are just as smart as other people. Some are smarter. Albert Einstein and Thomas Edison were both very smart men who did amazing things. They were also dyslexic! People who have dyslexia can be whatever they want to be. There are very **successful** (suk-SES-ful) doctors, writers, and teachers who are dyslexic. Even some famous people, such as actor Tom Cruise, are dyslexic.

◄ Everybody can be successful, whether they have dyslexia or not.

You're Not Alone

Dyslexic kids are smart and they like to have fun. All kids can improve at something. Some kids are great at playing the piano or shooting baskets. Other kids may not be good at music but can run really fast. Having dyslexia might make school hard, but it doesn't mean you're not smart. If you get help with your reading and writing, you can be great at anything you want.

Glossary

diagnose (dy-ug-NOHS) To figure out a problem by looking at signs and symptoms.

dyslexia (dis-LEK-see-uh) A condition that causes people to have trouble with reading, writing, or math.

dyslexic (dis-LEK-sik) A person with dyslexia.

frustrated (FRUS-tray-ted) When you feel angry or sad because you cannot do anything about a certain situation.

learning disability (LER-ning dis-uh-BIL-uh-tee) A condition that makes it hard for you to learn things.

organized (OR-guh-nyzd) To keep things neat and in order.

successful (suk-SES-ful) To finish a project or activity well.

Index